Time Management for a Productive Life

(Personal Development for Beginners #2)

Eddie de Jong

http://dejong.co.za

ISBN-13: 978-1496065391
ISBN-10: 1496065395

Contents

Introduction

"You control your future, your destiny. What you think about comes about. By recording your dreams and goals on paper, you set in motion the process of becoming the person you most want to be. Put your future in good hands - your own."

Mark Victor Hansen

"Life is GREAT" is an expression I frequently use. When I do, people will often look at me strangely and I can almost hear them thinking "what has this guy been drinking?" When someone asks me (often habitually) how I am, a favorite response of mine is "always good!" Once again, a strange look is a common reaction, often followed by comments along the lines of "you must really have a good life if you say that" or "is that even possible?"

I don't say those thing as a conversational gimmick or in an effort to convince myself. I say them because that is honestly how I feel, and how I experience life. Don't get me wrong - I'm not saying that I don't have ups and downs, good times as well as bad. I do. That's normal, every human being on our planet has them. What I am however saying, is that happiness and being excited about life, and its endless wonders and possibilities, is both a choice and a state of mind.

In my teenage years, I was an extreme introvert with no social skills whatsoever. My reality existed only in my head and, although I lived in an external world, it had very little impact on me. If I think back today, there is actually very little that I remember from my school days. At the same time, I was an avid reader.

My mother would take us to the public library once a week, and we were all allowed to borrow three books.

By the next visit, I had not only read my own and my two siblings' books, but had also checked if my mother had something that I could read. This meant that I read an average of nine to twelve books per week.

If any subject interested me, it was therefore logical to find a book with the information and learn from it. I still remember *"Popular Mechanics"* and the hours of fun I had exploring all the fascinating subjects this great series contained. Another learning activity for me was to take things apart to see how they worked. More often than not, there were 'spares' left over after I had put the items back together (much to my mother's frustration), but I could generally get them to work again.

This love of books and learning has stayed with me throughout my life. Computers weren't around during my school days, but when I 'discovered' them, I taught myself how to program using books. What started as a hobby became a career, and I soon ran my own software development company – not bad for someone without any formal training in computers or programming!

How did I manage to go from a technician to owning a company that developed strategically important software for large Petrochemical companies? Yes, you guessed it – by setting goals and sticking to them, learning about time management and developing good habits.

When my kids were still at home, I read *Seven Habits of Highly Effective People* (http://tinyurl.com/oktazol) and later *The 7 Habits of Highly Effective Families* (http://tinyurl.com/pz9rdyl).

These books were a breakthrough for me, as in them, I finally found the principles that I could teach others.

This also led to me formulating my own personal mission statement:

"I will help people become the best that they can be."

The reason I'm telling you this is simply to assure you that the techniques and processes I'm going to describe in the chapters that follow, are not some theoretical mumbo jumbo. I have used these methods and seen the results – they work! Fortunately, I am hardheaded and thick skinned enough not to listen to the doomsayers.

Amongst many other things, I am a certified Life Coach. The very first session that we do with our clients teaches them how to set effective goals. Time and again I see a transformation taking place. There is no bigger satisfaction than seeing when someone suddenly realizes: **"I can do this!"**

Make no mistake – reaching your goals and gradually designing and building the life that you want is hard work. There are no short cuts. There is no easy way. This is not some magic formula that will change your life overnight.

BUT ...

If you are willing to pay the price, I will show you how you can make your dreams come true.

Are you ready to take action and change your life forever?

"Ever since I was a child I have had this instinctive urge for expansion and growth. To me, the function and duty of a quality human being is the sincere and honest development of one's potential."

Bruce Lee

Everyone has an instinctive urge for expansion and growth. Personality traits such as being an introvert or extrovert has nothing to do with it, nor is reading personal development books the only way by which a person can develop and grow.

In our society, personal growth starts when we go to school, or even before that, when we learn to walk and talk. Learning new things in your work environment, being coached or even doing the coaching – all these activities lead to a person growing. We all grow in some way or another.

The level of awareness of this growth, and the conscious thought and effort that goes into it, do however often determine the direction and ultimately, the level of achievement or success that is reached.

Any study of successful people will reveal that they don't simply 'go with the flow'. They know (often from an early age) what they want, and then actively go out and get it.

When I tutor school kids, I am often frustrated by their unwillingness to use the opportunities with which they are presented. Here they are in a private school, but they couldn't be bothered to pay attention in class or do homework. I don't think that this attitude is limited to the youth. Many grown-ups simply don't realize that they can determine their own future. They never take responsibility for their lives, but constantly blame others, or make excuses for their 'misfortune', when it is often a direct result of their actions (or in-actions).

"The consuming desire of most human beings is deliberately to plant their whole life in the hands of some other person. I would describe this method of searching for happiness as immature. Development of character consists solely in moving toward self-sufficiency."

Quentin Crisp

This Personal Development for Beginners series of books won't help you believe in yourself, nor can they force you to take action. Those elements can only come from deep within you.

"You can have all the tools in the world but if you don't genuinely believe in yourself, it's useless."

Ken Jeong

Having said that, if you do believe in yourself and are prepared to pay the price, but don't know where to start, this series was written for you.

As you will have noticed, each book is short and (hopefully) to the point. Each book also stands on its own – you can read only one book without having to read the others. I have tried to make them concise, but practical at the same time. An old Chinese proverb says *"A journey of a thousand miles starts with one small step."*

I hope that you will take that first small step with me. If you do, I can assure you that it will be the start of a journey that is spectacular and exhilarating at the same time.

"We would accomplish many more things if we did not think of them as impossible."

Eddie de Jong

Why manage your time?

"Lost wealth may be replaced by industry, lost knowledge by study, lost health by temperance or medicine, but lost time is gone forever."

Samuel Smiles

I'm sure you have heard the expression *"Time is Money"*, or even used it yourself.

The phrase was originally used by Benjamin Franklin in "Advice to a Young Tradesman". Nowadays, it is commonly taken to mean (My) time is valuable, so don't waste it.

We all have the same amount of time every day – whether you choose to count it in hours, minutes or seconds. In spite of this, some people are much more productive, and get much more done in a day than others.

Although Time Management is often associated with the work and business environments, using our time effectively is something we can all benefit from. Whether you are a student, or retired like I am, knowing simple time management techniques will help you bring balance to your life.

The well-known Biblical quote "There is a time for everything..." unfortunately does not say "There is time for everything". Time is a scarce and valuable resource, just like money is. I would even go as far as to say that time is more valuable than money. The quote above says it all: "Lost time is gone forever." This book will teach you how to use your time wisely.

People often think that retirees have all the time in the world. I can assure you that this is not the case. I spend my days writing, tutoring, coaching, gardening, doing maintenance around the house, exercising and cooking. Then there is time spent with my family and friends, church activities and publishing and marketing my books. On top of all this, I read an average of about 100 books per year, and write reviews for these on Amazon. My reading is a mixture of fiction and non-fiction, with the latter currently focused on how to improve my writing, publishing and marketing.

The reason I'm telling you this is simply to assure you that the techniques and processes I'm going to describe in the chapters that follow are not some theoretical mumbo jumbo. I have used these methods and seen the results – they work!

Are you ready to take action and change your life forever?

Timesheets

"Don't be fooled by the calendar. There are only as many days in the year as you make use of. One man gets only a week's value out of a year while another man gets a full year's value out of a week."

Charles Richards

When I was still working in the corporate world, I would occasionally have to fill in timesheets. Although I understood why it was necessary, *I hated having to do this!*

If you want to manage your time better, it means that you will have to make changes in your life. Change is after all what personal development is all about. During this process, there may very well be things that you have to do, but don't enjoy. The choice is actually very simple – **do what you need to and you will achieve results, or don't.**

Before deciding what it is that we want to change in our life, it is often beneficial to stand back and look at our life as it is currently.

In Goal Setting for Success (http://tinyurl.com/ltufl4q), the first book in this personal development series, we use a Life Wheel or look at different areas or roles in our life to determine where we are currently, and where changes are most required.

Managing time is actually a lot like managing your money. Before you can set a meaningful budget with money, you need to know the amounts you are receiving and what you are spending it on. Only once you know this in detail can you decide where changes are required or even possible.

The timesheet is the budget of time management. Some books also refer to this as a time journal. Irrespective of its name, the purpose is the same. Your first step in managing your time is to start tracking what you spend your time on.

Choose a method and a format that is comfortable for you. You might want to use an old-fashioned notepad and pen / pencil. Using an app on your tablet or smart phone will most likely be more appealing to the younger generation. How you do it isn't important – the fact that you keep track is. The method you use must however work for you and be easy to do for it to be sustainable.

The first thing to record would be your sleeping time. Sleep is important, but the amount of sleep people need varies. I know that I need a solid eight hours per night. My wife on the other hand, is a chronic insomniac and gets by on four to six hours per night. Recording the amount you sleep will allow you to later reduce the time in favor of more productive activities, if possible.

The more detail you record, the better. More detail means that you will be able to really hone in and fine-tune your use of time. It does however also mean that more time is required to do the capturing. Somewhere in between the extremes lies a balance. You need to find the road that will give you the most value for your specific circumstances.

To limit the time spent on the actual capturing, feel free to use your own abbreviations. Just make sure you understand what they mean afterward. Nobody else has to be able to read your timesheet, but if you can't, all your effort will have been wasted.

It might very well be good enough to book one hour per day for lunch, and leave it at that. Recording what you had for lunch and how long you had to wait in the queue won't add any value. If you however in reality only spend 30 minutes of that hour in actually getting and consuming your food and the other 30 minutes is spent gazing at pigeons in the park, this is worth recording.

At the end of the day, you could decide that pigeon gazing is a required activity for you to relax and keep it in your schedule, or you could decide to use those 30 minutes in a different way.

If you had however only recorded one hour for lunch and left it at that, you would have missed out on the opportunity to add additional productivity to your day.

I recommend that you log your time for at least two weeks. Our lives tend to follow the same pattern week in and week out, so recording the first week's activities should give you a clear picture of where change is possible. In the second week, you should already be making changes, so it should look different than your first "raw" week.

As you make the changes, keeping track of your days on a continuous basis is a good idea anyway – how else will you know if you are on track? Once you know what you are spending your time on, I recommend that you repeat the exercise for a week every month. We often start with a new idea or making changes very enthusiastically but, as time goes by, there is a tendency to lose focus. Doing a reality check every month will allow you to easily get back on track if it is required.

A timesheet is the budget of Time Management.

Action steps:

1. Choose a method that you are going to be using for your time-sheet.

2. Start keeping track of your time *right now*, even before you start reading the next chapter.

3. Capture as much detail as possible without overloading yourself. Use abbreviations where possible.

4. In the beginning, work out a system to remind you to fill in your timesheet. Maybe a reminder on your calendar every hour could work?

Which activities are most important?

"Most of us spend too much time on what is urgent and not enough time on what is important."

Stephen R. Covey

When you do your budget, chances are you won't have enough money to do everything you want to. A common technique used to decide what to spend money on, is to distinguish between **needs** and **wants**.

Needs would typically include things like rent, food and utilities (electricity, gas and water).

Wants could be things like going to the movies, buying new toys for the kids or buying the latest smart phone.

It is important to realize that needs and wants will be unique for every person.

Men typically classify chocolate as a want, but I know many women who are adamant that it is a need! Jokes aside, only **you** can decide where the balance lies for you. It is after all **your** life we're talking about here.

The same principle applies to time; although it might be less obvious which activities are more important than others. For years, I prioritized my activities with a simple numbering system with activities marked with a one or an A being the most important, two or B being less important and so on.

In his book, *Seven Habits of Highly Effective People* (http://tinyurl.com/oktazol), **Stephen Covey** uses the four quadrants as shown below to classify activities.

1 Urgent and Important	2 not Urgent but Important
3 Urgent but not Important	4 Neither Urgent nor Important

Although it might look obvious at first glance, I would first like to discuss typical activities in each quadrant:

Urgent and Important activities are those that **must** be done as soon as possible. If they're not done, the consequences are normally negative. If your geyser at home bursts, you had better get it fixed as soon as possible. If you leave it for later, the water damage to ceilings, furniture and carpets could get worse, and you would have to take cold showers or baths.

In the business environment, if your manager gives you a specific task with a deadline, and you don't have much time to do the job, it has to become a 1st quadrant activity.

Not delivering on time might get you fired. On the other hand, if your manager gives you the same job, but there is still plenty of time to do it, the job would move to quadrant two – not Urgent but important.

Spending too much time doing quadrant one activities leads to undue stress and is best avoided if possible. A geyser bursting can't be planned for, but many routine maintenance tasks that would fall in quadrant two can, if done properly, prevent quadrant one activities. One example of this is servicing your car. It would normally fall in quadrant two but, if not done, could lead to breakdowns which would push you into quadrant one.

In an ideal world, **quadrant two** is where you want to spend most of your time. Typical examples of quadrant two activities for me would be writing, and spending quality time with my wife.

Unfortunately, quadrant two activities often get neglected precisely because they are not urgent. This will happen if you don't manage your time properly, and either get inundated with 'fire-fighting' emergencies (quadrant one), or wasting time with quadrant three and four activities.

A crucial element to get this right is for you to decide what is important to you, and not to get hi-jacked by other people's 'urgency'.

As we don't live in a perfect world, try and spend at least 80% of your time doing quadrant 2 activities

Urgent but not important activities are often difficult to identify. It does in fact sound like an oxymoron doesn't it? How can something that is not important be urgent? Most often, the perceived urgency is either created as a result of social conditioning, or is someone else's urgency that you don't have to make your own.

Eddie de Jong

When my kids were still living at home, I had a rule that we all had supper together around the dining room table (a quadrant two activity). If the phone rang during that time, it was not to be answered. In the beginning, the kids had a hard time accepting this and tried arguments such as "But it could be important!"

Think about this. If there is a crisis somewhere that you have to deal with, will another 10, 20 or even 30 minutes make such a difference? With all the times that we did not answer the phone during supper, it **never** happened that there was a crisis that would have been solved easier if we had answered the phone. Most of the time the call was made by either a telemarketer or occasionally it was one of the kid's friends.

Either case could be handled later, without any urgency or even importance at all. I did in fact notice an unplanned benefit to this rule - many telemarketers call around supper time as this is when most people are at home. I suspect that not answering the phone resulted in many 'pesky' calls that went unanswered. With automatic answering systems and caller identification on many phones nowadays, this rule makes even more sense. If it is urgent, people will leave a message.

Answering your phone during a meeting and constantly reacting to social media are two more examples where people have not really thought about their priorities, and somehow define these activities as urgent.

Take a moment right now, sit back and ask yourself the questions: "Are these really urgent activities that you have to do right now? What would happen if I don't answer the phone or react to social media right now?"

Years ago, I read a notice on the wall of a major oil company:

*Bad Management on **YOUR** behalf does not constitute a crises in **MY** life.*

Although the grammar might not be correct, I have always loved the meaning.

I worked for a small, two-man company with only the MD /owner and myself. The MD had visited a customer two weeks earlier and had agreed on software changes that I had to implement. They had agreed that the changes would be delivered within three weeks.

The MD had forgotten to tell me about these changes, and only informed me one week before the deadline. To achieve this, I would have had to work for seven days, 18 hours per day. At the time, I was enrolled in night classes in business school. Trying to deliver the project on time would mean that I would not be able to attend the classes that week and I would be letting down the other team members in our study group.

After much deliberation and internal struggles, I informed the MD that I would not be delivering the project on time. I would give everything during normal working hours, but would not compromise the things I felt were important in order to fix his mistake.

Although this decision damaged our relationship and ultimately led to us parting ways, I have not regretted it for a single moment.

Completing the night classes was part of **my** dream and ultimately enabled me to start my own software development company.

Fourth quadrant activities are often disguised as relaxation. Don't get me wrong here – taking time to relax is crucial and forms an integral part of leading a balanced life. Do yourself a favor and look at your relaxation activities critically. It is often not simply a case of what you do, but more importantly, how much of it do you do.

My personal Achilles' heel is playing Spider Solitaire. If I don't watch myself, I could spend hours playing. Computer games and watching TV are probable the main time wasters in our society today. Be aware of, and limit the time you spend on such mindless activities.

Eddie de Jong

Jeff Olson tells a story of a shoe cleaning lady at an airport in his book, _The Slight Edge_ (http://tinyurl.com/peox6fu). This lady read piles and piles of cheap novels to while away the time in between customers. Jeff poses the question: "What difference would it have made to this lady's life if she had read 10 pages per day of nonfiction, personal development books, instead of the fiction she was devouring?"

If she had done that, she would have moved from spending most of her time in quadrant four (neither Urgent nor Important) to quadrant two (not Urgent but Important).

Do you regularly spend time in quadrant three or four? If so, now is the time to look at those activities and replace them with quadrant two activities.

If you are looking for a book to help you become more productive or effective, do yourself a favor and buy **Jeff Olson's** _The Slight Edge_ (http://tinyurl.com/peox6fu). In my view, this is the best personal development book I've ever read. I can guarantee that it will improve the quality of your life if you apply the easy principles outlined in it.

Once you understand which activities belong in each quadrant, take your timesheet and prioritize your activities according to the quadrants. In the next chapter, we will look at how to plan your time so that you can become as effective as you can be.

Action steps:

1. Take your timesheet and classify all the activities according to the four quadrants.

2. Look at quadrant one activities and think about how you can prevent them from becoming urgent in future.

3. Look at quadrant three and four activities and either cut them out completely or replace them with quadrant two activities.

Can you already see that you have more time available for the important thing in your life?

Eddie de Jong

Organizing your day

"He who every morning plans the transaction of the day and follows out that plan, carries a thread that will guide him through the maze of the most busy life. But where no plan is laid, where the disposal of time is surrendered merely to the chance of incidence, chaos will soon reign."

Victor Hugo

When things in your life seem almost too much to handle, when 24 hours in a day are not enough, remember the mayonnaise jar and two beers.

A professor stood before his philosophy class and had some items in front of him. When the class began, wordlessly, he picked up a very large and empty mayonnaise jar and started to fill it with golf balls.

He then asked the students if the jar was full. They agreed that it was.

The professor then picked up a box of pebbles and poured it into the jar. He shook the jar lightly. The pebbles rolled into the open areas between the golf balls.

He then asked the students again if the jar was full. They agreed it was.

The professor next picked up a box of sand and poured it into the jar. Of course, the sand filled up everything else. He asked once more if the jar was full.

The students responded with a unanimous 'yes.'

The professor then produced two pints of beer from under the table and poured the entire contents into the jar, effectively filling the empty space between the sand. The students laughed.

'Now,' said the professor, as the laughter subsided, 'I want you to recognize that this jar represents your life.

The golf balls are the important things - God, family, children, health, friends, and favorite passions. Things, that if everything else was lost and only they remained, your life would still be full.

The pebbles are the things that matter like your job, house, and car.

The sand is everything else: the small stuff.'

'If you put the sand into the jar first,' he continued, 'there is no room for the pebbles or the golf balls. The same goes for life. If you spend all your time and energy on the small stuff, you will never have room for the things that are important to you.

So... Pay attention to the things that are critical to your happiness:

Know your God.
Play with your children.
Take time to get medical check-ups.
Take your partner out to dinner.

There will always be time to clean the house and fix the dripping tap. Take care of the golf balls first: the things that really matter.

Set your priorities. The rest is just sand.'

One of the students raised her hand and inquired what the beers represented.

The professor smiled. 'I'm glad you asked'. It just goes to show you that no matter how full your life may seem, there's always room for a couple of beers with a friend.'

Source Unknown

The golf balls in the story above represent your first quadrant activities and the pebbles are second quadrant activities. When you start out with planning your time properly, it is likely that you'll find that you have a fair number of quadrant one activities.

Don't worry if at first you don't have much time for quadrant two activities, the place where you really want to be spending most of your time.

When you schedule your day or week, fit in these activities first. While doing so, examine your quadrant one (urgent and important) activities critically, and decide if they are really as urgent and / or as important as you first thought. If they are, great – give them first priority and get them out of the way.

Once all the quadrant one activities have been scheduled, fill in the gaps with quadrant two activities, then quadrant three and lastly fill the remainder of your time with the "neither urgent nor important" stuff.

WAIT!

Do you really want to spend your precious time doing things that are neither urgent nor important?

Most of the time we tend to live our lives on "automatic", i.e. without really thinking about what we do and why.

If you followed my instructions above and filled the remainder of your time with stuff that is not important, you need to re-look your list and **ruthlessly cut out** those activities that are not taking you to the place you ultimately want to be. Perhaps you should look at the action steps at the end of the previous chapter?

Ultimately, you will still end up with a 'To Do" list that is prioritized. There is no getting away from it. The big difference is that you will now be focusing on the things that are important to **you**.

Your life will start changing and become ***YOUR*** *life*

Keeping track of all the things you need to do is tricky. You might have a list for the office and one for home. Interruptions that can't be ignored will happen and prevent you from getting everything done that you want to. This is normal and is to be expected.

Once again, you need to find a way of keeping track that works for you. It has to be comfortable and easy to do and might well combine different methods or systems. The important thing is to have everything written down or captured in some format – trying to remember everything just won't cut it.

One way to make sure you keep track and shuffle priorities is to block out time for this activity on a daily basis. Will first thing in the mornings work for you, or is before you go to bed better? Tick off activities as you complete them – not only does it keep your list up to date, but it also gives a great feeling of achievement.

Reorganizing your list regularly (weekly, monthly?) is also a good idea as, no matter which method you use to keep track, it will inevitably become messy at some stage.

Action steps:

1. Plan your day or week by prioritizing the important activities first.

2. Block out time to keep track and prioritize daily.

3. Regularly reorganize or re-write your list to keep it manageable.

Procrastination

"Procrastination is the foundation of all disasters."

Pandora Poikilos

Procrastination is actually very common. I think we all procrastinate at some stage in our lives. Before we look at how to overcome procrastination, try and figure out why you procrastinate. Sit back and think about a task that you keep on putting off. Why don't you **just do it**? (Thanks Nike) Answering "I don't feel like it" is not good enough. Why don't you feel like it?

If you really think about it, chances are that:

- The task is boring.

- You intensely dislike doing the task.

- The task is so big that you are not sure if you are capable of doing it.

When I was a kid, my mother had the rule that we had to eat everything that was served for dinner. If there was something that we didn't like, we would try everything to get away from having to eat it, but my mother was resolute. If you didn't finish the food, you stayed at the table no matter how long it took.

Once we had resigned ourselves to the fact that there was no getting around it, we would gobble up the 'yucky' food as fast as we could at the start of the meal, and then enjoy the rest at our leisure.

Years later, I learnt that **Mark Twain** said *"Eat a live frog first thing in the morning and nothing worse will happen to you the rest of the day."*

Procrastination normally doesn't make the task go away. Knowing that you have to do it but putting it off puts undue stress on you, and often leads to a quadrant two activity moving to quadrant one and becoming a crisis.

If the task is boring or you dislike doing it, get it out of the way as soon as possible and get it over and done with. An additional bonus will be less stress, not to mention the tremendous feeling of satisfaction of doing this. You could even reward yourself by doing something that you enjoy doing straight after you have completed your boring task.

Remember, ultimately **you** are in control of your life. This small change in mindset might well be one of the most rewarding you will ever experience.

For tasks that are huge and daunting, the technique is slightly different, but equally effective – break the task down into smaller tasks until it becomes small enough to manage comfortably.

"How do you eat an elephant?"
"One bite at a time."

Think about raising children. At first glance, it is a massive task and entails many, many different and often unknown action steps. Yet, many of us manage - one day at a time, or sometimes literally minute by minute.

Writing a book is another good example. Many would be authors never get started because of the sheer size of the undertaking. If you however write consistently for just one hour per day, the book will get written.

"The best time to start was last year. Failing that, today will do."

Chris Guillebeau

Action steps:

1. Identify the tasks that you keep on putting off.

2. Find the reason why you are avoiding doing certain tasks.

3. Take control - just do it or split the task into manageable chunks.

4. Celebrate as you achieve success in wiping out procrastination.

"Never leave 'till tomorrow which you can do today."

Benjamin Franklin

Eddie de Jong

Consistency

"Determine never to be idle. No person will have occasion to complain of the want of time who never loses any. It is wonderful how much can be done if we are always doing."

Thomas Jefferson

In his book *The Slight Edge* (http://tinyurl.com/peox6fu), **Jeff Olson** says: *"Showing up is important, but its natural companion consistency is what makes it a powerful duo. Showing up consistently is where the magic happens."*

Many years ago I was a technical manager for a company. One of the technicians, Dave, came to me with a problem.

"We are the same age and have the same qualifications, yet you are the technical manager and I am only a technician. Why is that?" he asked.

"Whatever I do, I give it my all and do the best I can," I answered. "Management noticed this and when a new position opened up, it was only natural for them to select me."

"But I can also do that. Give me a chance and I will prove myself."

No matter how I tried, I couldn't help him understand that it wasn't about being given an opportunity to show what you can do, and then do your best, but about doing your best irrespective of who is looking. That attitude leads to the opportunities. This is consistency at work.

Consistently doing the things that are important to you, no matter what the circumstances, is the **key** to achieving success and personal development. If we start with something and then stop, it is often difficult to get going again. Think about it – why are Mondays often blue? We've had a break from our normal work, and getting into it again is difficult.

If you keep on doing the things that are important to you seven days a week, you will be much more productive than if you take the weekend off. I am not saying that you should never relax, but even relaxing can be done by doing things that are important.

If personal development is important to you, you might want to consider doing it even on weekends. You might reduce the time spent on these activities, but do it anyway. Try it and you will be amazed at how much faster you can reach your goals.

Even times that are normally not productively used can become meaningful. How much time do you spend commuting, standing in queues or waiting for others? Instead of being bored and unproductive, look at your short activities in quadrant two and see if you can fit them in. I always have my Kindle with me, and when I have to wait, I read nonfiction. Using an iPod to listen to motivational or personal development talks while driving or exercising is another way that you could use to consistently improve yourself.

Have to send 10 000 emails to customers? Instead of blocking off one chunk of time to do this, split the job into five or ten minute sections. You can then do these when you have those in-between moments with nothing else to do instead of playing computer games or randomly surfing the web. Call a friend a day, every day. Be creative. Think of new ways to be consistent.

"I like to do weird things in the shower, like drink my coffee, brush my teeth and drink a smoothie. It's good time management."

Michelle Williams

I watched the movie "Zero Dark Thirty" last night. In the scene where they are flying in with helicopters to kill Bin Laden, one of the soldiers is wearing earphones. When asked by another soldier what he was listening to, he answered "Tony Robbins." That's what I call consistency! This soldier knew what he wanted to do with his life after being a soldier, and was using every opportunity he got to prepare for that day.

Action steps:

1. From your timesheet, identify your idle time, as well as the times that you are busy with mindless activity.

2. Fill these times with meaningful activities.

Eddie de Jong

Dealing with Interruptions

"The way we measure productivity is flawed. People checking their BlackBerry over dinner is not the measure of productivity."

Timothy Ferriss

Today more than ever, we have constant interruptions. With the Internet, email, computers and smart phones, there is never a moment that you can't be busy with something. Interruptions are destructive by nature. Not only do we have to deal with them, but once they have been removed, it takes precious time to pick up where you have left off on the activity you were busy with.

Although it might be difficult to believe, each interruption involves a choice. Interruptions that are self-imposed are relatively easy to deal with. An example of this would be when I'm busy writing. I write for a specific amount of time every day. If I'm busy, and I suddenly see that I have a new email, I can choose to look at the email immediately, thus disrupting what I'm doing, or I can ignore the email and look at it later, at a time specifically set aside for this.

External interruptions are often not as easy to ignore and you might well find that you need to communicate to people around you as to when interruptions are acceptable and when not. The question you need to ask yourself is this "In terms of where I want to go and what I want to become, is it really important that I do this **now**?" If the answer is "no", then don't do it.

When you are focusing on quadrant two activities, block out the time specifically for that and, where possible, switch off your computer and phone. Focus on the task at hand and get it done.

Multitasking does not work, unless you do a mindless physical activity like exercising or washing the dishes. In those cases you can multitask by listening to worthwhile material or thinking about and planning your next task.

I know that it is not always practical, especially in a work environment, to ignore all interrupts. If your boss demands your attention, you had better respond. In cases like that, pay attention to the interrupt and decide if you have to take action **now**. If the answer is "no" (and it will be more often than you think), simply note the new task and continue focusing on the task at hand.

For very long tasks that simply can't be done in one session, break it down into smaller pieces. After each section is done, check for emergencies or crises that needs your attention immediately. If there are any, handle them and then get back to the important stuff as soon as possible.

In the home environment, your spouse or kids might demand your attention at inconvenient times. Even here, simple discipline and communication can solve the problem. If your family knows that you are not to be interrupted at certain times, most, if not all of their emergencies will miraculously disappear or can be dealt with later.

By the same token, family time is important. As part of your scheduled, important activities, set aside time for the family. During those times, focus only on that activity - no checking of work emails or whatever else during family time!

Although it might be difficult to believe, each interruption involves a choice.

<u>Action steps:</u>

1. When you are working on a specific task, remove all sources of interruption where it is possible to do so.

2. When interruptions occur, question and choose whether or not you will or must respond **now**.

3. Communicate and negotiate interruption limits with the people surrounding you.

Eddie de Jong

Summary

"One reason so few of us achieve what we truly want is that we never direct our focus; we never concentrate our power. Most people dabble their way through life, never deciding to master anything in particular."

Tony Robbins

1. Choose a method that you are going to be using for your time-sheet.

2. Start keeping track of your time *right now.*

3. In the beginning, work out a system to remind you to fill in your timesheet.

4. Take your timesheet and classify all the activities according to the four quadrants.

5. Look at quadrant one activities and think about how you can prevent them from becoming urgent in future.

6. Look at quadrant three and four activities and either cut them out completely or replace them with quadrant two activities.

7. Plan your day or week by prioritizing the important activities first.

8. Identify the tasks that you keep on putting off.

9. Find the reason why you are avoiding doing certain tasks.

10. Take control - just do it or split the task into manageable chunks.

11. Celebrate as you achieve success in wiping out procrastination.

12. From your timesheet, identify your idle time, as well as the times that you are busy with mindless activity.

13. Fill these times with meaningful activities.

14. When you are working on a specific task, remove all sources of interruption where it is possible to do so.

15. When interruptions occur, question and choose whether or not you will or must respond **now**.

16. Communicate and negotiate interruption limits with the people surrounding you.

17. Regularly reorganize or re-write your list to keep it manageable.

Conclusion

"There are two primary choices in life: to accept conditions as they exist, or accept the responsibility for changing them."

Denis Waitley

As you start applying your new time management techniques and changing yourself and your life for the better, you will find people that have something negative to say about your goals or ambitions. I believe that the number one reason for people not becoming the best they can, is because others tell them, in whatever way, that they can't do it.

This is often not because people are inherently nasty, but is caused by ignorance. Many people don't realize that they can, to a certain degree, control their own future and destiny. They simply "go with the flow" and react unthinkingly to their environment and circumstances. People also tend to view life through their own narrow perspective, and simply fail to see the possibilities life itself offers us.

If you are doubted, criticized or even laughed at, remember that you do have a choice as to how you're going to react to this type of attitude.

You can either believe in them more than in yourself and sink slowly into the common pool of mediocrity, or you can decide to ignore the naysayers, put your head down and work on becoming the best you can.

I you decide on doing the latter, you will be in good company. History gives us a number of well-known examples of people that were scoffed at by their peers or 'betters', but who, in spite of this, rose above it to become world renown for their achievements.

Being from South Africa, the first example that comes to my mind is *Nelson Mandela*. From being found guilty of treason and sentenced to life imprisonment, to becoming South Africa's first democratically elected President, his journey became a legend and lifted his status to that of an international icon.

Searching for some more examples, I found a list mentioning people such as Thomas Edison, Albert Einstein and Abraham Lincoln. Each of these individuals had been told at some stage in their lives that they we not good enough, yet they went on to achieve greatness.

What made these people different? Put simply, they believed in themselves. They knew they always had a choice, and never gave up dreaming. However, dreaming in itself is not enough. Remember, to achieve your dreams, you have to take action and keep at it **no matter what happens**.

If the people mentioned on the list could achieve what they did, what is stopping you from achieving to best that you can be?

Twelve Famous People Who Succeeded Against the Odds.
(http://tinyurl.com/ku5qjyd)

1. **Thomas Edison,** the inventor of the light bulb, was told by his teacher that he was too stupid to learn anything.
2. **Louisa May Alcott,** author of Little Women, was turned down by countless publishers who told her no one would ever read her now classic children's book.
3. **Woodrow Wilson**, a Rhodes scholar and president of the United States, didn't learn the alphabet until he was eight; he didn't read until he was eleven.

4. **Wilma Rudolph** contracted polio at age four, crippling her as a child. She was told she would never walk. She decided to become a runner and went on to win three Olympic gold medals and was named the "Fastest Woman in the World."
5. **Albert Einstein** did not talk until age four or read until age nine He performed badly in almost all of his high school courses and failed his college entrance exams.
6. **Abraham Lincoln** began his service in the Blackhawk War as captain. By the end of the war he had been demoted to private.
7. **Lucille Ball** was told when she first started studying acting by an instructor to "Try any other profession. Any other."
8. **Ludwig van Beethoven** was initially told by his music teacher that he was hopeless as a composer.
9. **Cher** had learning disabilities as a child.
10. **Michael Jordan** was cut from his high school basketball team.
11. **Walt Disney** was fired by a newspaper editor for lacking great ideas. He went bankrupt several times and was told repeatedly to "get rid of the mouse because there's no potential in it."

Although the heading says twelve people, there were in fact only eleven mentioned on the list, but I'm sure you can add some more names if you feel so inclined.

Thanks for reading!

I write these books because I enjoy doing so, and I love to help people become the best they can be.

If you have enjoyed this book and have found value in it, won't you please consider leaving an honest review on Amazon?

Your review can help other potential readers make an informed decision on whether to buy this book or not.

Click here (http://tinyurl.com/odqsqhc) to review now.

PS. If you decide not to do a review for whatever reason, that's okay.

BUT

Don't you dare not take action on the new things you've learnt by reading this book!

You can change your life and make it what you want it to be,
but only if
you take consistent action.

Other books by Eddie de Jong

<u>Non-fiction</u>

1. Win with Excel
   (http://tinyurl.com/pup6awz)

2. Goal Setting for Success (Personal Development for Beginners # 1)
   (http://tinyurl.com/ltufl4q)

3. Time Management for a Productive Life (Personal Development for Beginners # 2)
   (http://tinyurl.com/pcomkml)

4. The Power of Habit: be Efficient in Everything you do (Personal Development for Beginners #3)
   (http://tinyurl.com/o5ez82b)

5. Personal Development for Beginners: Book 1 - 3: Goal Setting for Success; Time Management for a Productive Life; The Power of Habit: be Efficient in Everything you do
   (http://tinyurl.com/qfmgtqc)

6. Take Action! and Build the Life you want (Action for a better life #1)
   (http://amzn.to/1x3nlPg)

7. Take Action! and Start your own Business (Action for a better life #2)
   (http://amzn.to/1OJ7n5n)

Fiction

1. Velvak's Victory (Bradapol book #1)
   (http://tinyurl.com/q9m7yxh)

2. Velvak and the Bio (Bradapol book #2)
   (http://tinyurl.com/lzjjtx8)

Recommended reading

If you enjoyed this book, you might also enjoy these personal development books on Time Management:

1. Time Management 2.0: 15 Secrets of a Self-Made Millionaire for Getting Things Done (Coffee With A Millionaire Series) by **Hank Reardon** (http://tinyurl.com/lxp2s42)

2. How to Work for Yourself: 100 Ways to Make the Time, Energy and Priorities to Start a Business, Book or Blog by **Bryan Cohen** (http://tinyurl.com/q2b2z8f)

3. Manage Your Day-to-Day: Build Your Routine, Find Your Focus, and Sharpen Your Creative Mind (The 99U Book Series) by **Jocelyn K. Glei** (http://tinyurl.com/nkypua5)

4. How to Live on 24 Hours a Day by **Arnold Bennett** (http://tinyurl.com/owyb2by)

5. The Productive Person: A how-to guide book filled with productivity hacks & daily schedules for entrepreneurs, students or anyone struggling with work-life balance by **James Roper** (http://tinyurl.com/q64h6qt)

6. Eat That Frog!: 21 Great Ways to Stop Procrastinating and Get More Done in Less Time by **Brian Tracy** (http://tinyurl.com/qjbzr49)

7. Organizing For Dummies by Eileen Roth
8. (http://tinyurl.com/k8rtqbp)

9. Time Management (The Brian Tracy Success Library) by
   Brian Tracy
   (http://tinyurl.com/lpz2a6w)

10. 21 Days To A More Disciplined Life by **Crystal Paine**
    (http://tinyurl.com/nxx6bzo)

11. Organizing from the Inside Out, second edition: The
    Foolproof System For Organizing Your Home, Your Office
    and Your Life by **Julie Morgenstern**
    (http://tinyurl.com/q2uqjgr)

www.ingramcontent.com/pod-product-compliance
Lightning Source LLC
Chambersburg PA
CBHW071824170526
45167CB00003B/1413